Bảo Anh Lạc Bookshelf 69

THE BLESSING CEREMONY FOR THE DECEASED

Composed
by

Bhikṣuṇī TN Giới Hương

Hong Duc Publishing

HUONG SEN BUDDHIST TEMPLE
19865 Seaton Avenue
Perris, CA 92570, USA
Tel: 951-657-7272, Cell: 951-616-8620
Email: huongsentemple@gmail.com
thichnugioihuong@yahoo.com
https://www.facebook.com/Huong.Sen.Riverside
Web: www.huongsentemple.com

THE FIRST WORDS

Every day Nuns and Buddhists at Hương Sen Buddhist Temple, California, USA, have practiced and recited following the Vietnamese scripture, "Nghi Lễ Hàng Ngày – 50 Kinh Tụng và các Lễ Vía trong Năm" (Daily Chanting – Fifty Discourses and Annual Festivals) of the Pureland Sect, which was composed in 2021 by Bhikkhunī Thích Nữ Giới Hương. It is based on the original ritual of her late Master, the Venerable Elder Hải Triều Âm at Liên Hoa Temple and Dược Sư Temple.[1]

Since many Vietnamese-Americans, Hispanic, native Americans, and English speakers have come to Huong Sen Temple in search of practice and ritual, Bhikkhunī Giới Hương composed an English version of **DAILY MONASTIC CHANTING**. It encompasses 16 popular rituals to serve the spiritual needs of any Buddhist sect, including the Pure Land and Meditation Traditions as below:

1. Practice Meditation
2. The Ceremony for Peace
3. The Rice Offering to Buddhas
4. The Lunch Offering at the Dining Hall
5. The Ritual Offering Food To Hungry Ghosts
6. The Pureland Course of Amitabha Sutra
7. The Medicine Buddha Sutra
8. The New Year Ceremony

---

1 Please read: http://www.huongsentemple.com/index.php/vn/phat-phap/kinh-ta-ng-ca-a-cha-a-hs/6256-nghi-le-hang-ngay-20.

9. The Great Parinirvana Ceremony
10. The Buddha's Birthday Ceremony
11. The Ullambana Festival (Parents' Day)
12. The Marriage Ceremony
13. The Blessing Ceremony for The Deceased
14. The Ancestral Ceremony
15. The Enlightened Buddha Ceremony
16. The Uposatha Ceremony (Reciting Precepts)

With regard to mindful chanting, we take sources from the sacred book, Chanting from the Heart: Buddhist Ceremonies and Daily Practices of Thích Nhất Hạnh. In the field of the Pureland School, we have taken material from the above Vietnamese scripture, "Nghi Lễ Hàng Ngày," and translated it into English.

We should chant at least once a week, any place and any time, or more often if we have more time. The chant will help to avoid negative thoughts, defilements, distractions -any of the myriad things that intrude into the one-pointed mind. We definitely feel the connectedness with Dharma (the Buddha's teaching), we feel the spirit being lifted up, the awakening and the settling of the mind to enter meditation. We will become bright, enduring, detached, diligent, generous, loving, understanding and so on . . . because we practice following the chanting and the role model of Buddhas.

Chanting out loud or silently listening to chanting can also be very relaxing as we go about our day. It can be used to calm our mind before work or sleeping.

For the sake of all the general practitioners, there are some changes, combinations, additions, reductions, and creations made in this English version. This is the first time that both traditions have been combined in an English version for the necessary needs at Huong Sen Buddhist Temple.

We would like to gratefully acknowledge with special thanks the Buddhas, Boddhisattvas, Sanghas, the English translators, Master Thích Nhất Hạnh, our Late Respectful Teacher - Venerable Elder Bhikkhunī Hải Triều Âm and others. You all provided us the awakening words to remind and guide us in the right way of practice. We will keep chanting, learning and practicing it until we and all beings get the enlightenment as well as realize our Buddha nature.

If there is any merit in compiling this book, may it be shared with all sentient beings. May they diligently practice and soon gain the way of love and understanding.

Reciting the sutras, practicing the way of awareness
gives rise to benefits without limit.
We vow to share the fruits with all beings.
We vow to offer tribute to parents, teachers, friends,
and numerous beings who
give guidance and support along the path.
(Thích Nhất Hạnh)

Hương Sen Temple, Riverside, California
March 15, 2023
Bhikkhunī TN Giới Hương

THE BLESSING CEREMONY FOR THE DECEASED

This ceremony includes the Blessing for the Deceased, Closing the Coffin, the Bury, the Cremation, the Seventh and Forty-ninth Days, the dead anniversaries, and so on. The leader can flexibly perform to change or add the needs accoding to the circumstances, customs, traditions and times. This ritual provides the basis.

At a temple, funeral home or a cemetary, a photograph of the deceased should be placed on the altar/table with his/her full name, Dharma name, the dates of birth and death and the longevity... Food, fruilt, flowers, candles should be placed in front of his/her photograph. It is better, if the food should be vegetarian.

1. Introduction (condolences and guidance)
2. The incense offering
3. Salutation
    3.1. Gratitude the Buddhas and Bodhisattvas
    3.2. Gratitude the Buddhas in the past
    3.3. Gratitude the Arahats
    3.4. Gratitude the Ancestors
4. The repentance gatha

5. Opening verse
6. Contemplation on no-coming, no-going
7. Beginning anew
8. Consecration of water
9. Reflecting on water
10. The Amitabha Sutra (if you have time)
11. The insight that brings us to the other shore
12. Read the Names of the Buddhas and Bodhisattvas
13. Taking refuge in the Amitabha Buddha
14. May the day and the night be well
15. Think of the deceased
16. Gatha on Impermanence
17. Prayer for the deceased
18. Salutation thousands of Buddhas in three times
19. The refuge chant
20. Taking refuge at three jewels
21. Sharing the merit & verse for closing
22. Words of gratitude.

***

1. INTRODUCTORY

Leader: **Today we are** (Bhikkhuni...)... **from... Temple to come... the funeral home..., at.... to take part the prayer for the deceased.**

First of all, we sincerely send our condolences and the sadness to you (families, relatives and friends of the deceased...) **for your loss.**

Secondly, we have gathered to recite and practice the sutras, to invoke the Buddhas' and Bodhisattvas' names, make offerings, and transfer the merits to the deceased (the full name, the Dharma name, longevity…) **on the ceremony of entering coffin/ closing coffin/ moving coffin/ cremation/ bury, the Seventh/ Forty-ninth Days or the dead anniversary… of the deceased. The children, relatives, and friends of the deceased are here to take part in the ceremony.**

We ask the community to listen with a quiet mind. Parents and grandparents, whether they are still alive or have left this life, are present in their children and grandchildren. The life of children and grandchildren is the life of the parents and the grandparents. The life of the ancestors carries on in the life of the children and grandchildren. According to the teaching of the Buddha, the peace and joy of the children and grandchildren are the peace and joy of the

parents, grandparents, and all ancestors. With a feeling of calm, clarity, and peace, we will make possible the calm, clarity, and peace of those who have left this life.

Please will the children, grandchildren, relatives and friends of the deceased (the full name, the Dharma name, longevity…) **stand before the Three Jewels, join your palms and pay homage to the Amitabha Buddhas, Buddhas and Bodhisattvas and ancestors.**

Please let us be aware of our present and the good fortune we have to be together today, offering all our love and support to the deceased and to each other during these profound moments of transformation.

Namo Amitabha Buddhaya. (ooo)

2.THE INCENSE OFFERING

Leader: **In gratitude, we offer this incense to all Buddhas and Bodhisattvas throughout space and time.**

May it be fragrant as Earth herself, reflecting our careful efforts, our wholehearted mindfulness, and the fruit of understanding, slowly ripening.

May we and all beings be companions of Buddhas and Bodhisattvas.

May we awaken from forgetfulness and realize our true home. (o)

Namo Offering the Incense
Bodhisattva Mahasattva. (3 times) (ooo)

3. SALUTATION IN GRATITUDE

(All Sangha members read)

3. 1. GRATITUDE THE BUDDHAS & BODDHISATTVAS

1. **Offering light in the Ten Directions, the Buddha, the Dharma, and the Sangha, to whom we bow in gratitude.** (o) (1 prostration)
2. **Teaching and living the way of awareness in the very midst of suffering and confusion, Shakyamuni Buddha, the Fully Enlightened One, to whom we bow in gratitude.** (o) (1 prostration)
3. **Cutting through ignorance, awakening our hearts and our minds, Manjushri, the Bodhisattva of Great Understanding, to whom we bow in gratitude.** (o) (1 prostration)
4. **Working mindfully, working joyfully for the sake of all beings, Samantabhadra, the Bodhisattva of Great Action, to whom we bow in gratitude.** (o) (1 prostration)
5. **Seed of awakening and loving kindness in**

children and all beings, Maitreya, the Buddha to-be-born, to whom we bow in gratitude. (o) (1 prostration)

6. **SeeingtheBuddhaineveryone,Sadaparibhuta, the Bodhisattva of Constant Respect, to whom we bow in gratitude.** (o) (1 prostration)
7. **Showing the way fearlessly and compassionately, the stream of all our Ancestral Teachers, to whom we bow in gratitude.** (ooo) (1 prostration)

3.2. GRATITUDE THE BUDDHAS IN THE PAST

1. **The Buddha Vipashyin, to whom we bow in gratitude.** (o) (1 prostration)
2. **The Buddha Shikhin, to whom we bow in gratitude.** (o) (1 prostration)

   The Buddha Vishvabhu, to whom we bow in gratitude. (o) (1 prostration)
3. **The Buddha Krakkucchandha, to whom we bow in gratitude.** (o) (1 prostration)
4. **The Buddha Konagamana, to whom we bow in gratitude.** (o) (1 prostration)
5. **The Buddha Kashyapa, to whom we bow in gratitude.** (o) (1 prostration)
6. **The Buddha Shakyamuni, to whom we bow**

in gratitude. (o) (1 prostration)

7. **The Bodhisattva of Great Understanding, Manjushri, to whom we bow in gratitude.** (o) (1 prostration)
8. **The Bodhisattva of Great Action, Samantabhadra, to whom we bow in gratitude.** (o) (1 prostration)
9. **The Bodhisattva of Great Compassion, Avalokiteshvara, to whom we bow in gratitude.** (ooo) (1 prostration)
10. **The Bodhisattva of the Great Vow, Kshitigarbha, to whom we bow in gratitude.** (ooo) (1 prostration)

3.3. GRATITUDE THE ARAHATS

1. **The Venerable Kashyapa, to whom we bow in gratitude.** (o) (1 prostration)
2. **The Venerable Shariputra, to whom we bow in gratitude.** (o) (1 prostration)
3. **The Venerable Maudgalyayana, to whom we bow in gratitude.** (o) (1 prostration)
4. **The Venerable Upali, to whom we bow in gratitude.** (o) (1 prostration)
5. **The Venerable Ananda, to whom we bow in gratitude.** (ooo) (1 prostration)

3. 4. GRATITUDE THE ANCESTORS

1. **Mother of Buddhas, Bodhisattvas, and all beings, nourishing, holding, and healing all, Bodhisattva Gaia, Great Mother Earth, precious jewel of the cosmos, to whom we bow in gratitude.** (o) (1 prostration)
2. **Radiating light in all directions, source of life on Earth, Mahavairocana Tathagata, Great Father Sun, Buddha of infinite light and life, to whom we bow in gratitude.** (o) (1 prostration)
3. **Seed of awakening and loving kindness in children and all beings, Maitreya, the Buddha to-be-born, to whom we bow in gratitude.** (o) (1 prostration)
4. **Showing the way fearlessly and compassionately, the stream of all our Ancestral Teachers, to whom we bow in gratitude.** (ooo) (1 prostration)

4. THE REPENTANCE GATHA

All wrongdoing arises from the mind.
When the mind is purified, what trace of wrong is left?
After repentance, my heart is light like the white clouds
that have always floated over the ancient forest

in freedom. (o)

Namo the Repentance
Bodhisattva Mahasattvas. (3 times) (ooo)

5. OPENING VERSE

The Dharma is deep and lovely.
We now have a chance to see, study, and practice it.
We vow to realize its true meaning.

Namo Shakyamunaye Buddhaya. (3 times) (ooo)

6. CONTEMPLATION ON NO-COMING, NO-GOING

This body is not me.
I am not limited by this body.
I am life without boundaries.
I have never been born,
and I have never died.

Look at the ocean and the sky filled with stars, manifestations from my wondrous True Mind. Since before time, I have been free.

Birth and death are only doors through which we pass, sacred thresholds on our journey.

Birth and death are a game of hide-and-seek. So laugh with me, hold my hand, let us say good-

bye, say good-bye, to meet again soon.

We meet today.
We will meet again tomorrow.
We will meet at the source every moment.
We meet each other in all forms of life. (o)

Namo Shakyamunaye Buddhaya. (3 times) (ooo)

7. BEGINNING ANEW

With great respect, we turn towards the conqueror of afflictions,
offering heartfelt words of repentance.
We have lived in forgetfulness for a long time.
As we have not had the opportunity to encounter the Dharma,
our habit energies have led us into suffering.
We have made many mistakes out of unskillfulness.
We have been blinded by our wrong perceptions for a very long time.
Our heart's garden is sown with attachment, hatred, and pride.
In us are seeds of killing, stealing, sexual misconduct, and lies.
Our everyday deeds and words do damage.
All these wrong actions are obstacles to our peace and joy.
Let us begin anew. (o)

**We see that we have been thoughtless,
straying from the path of mindfulness.
We have stored up afflictions and ignorance,
which have brought about so much aversion and sorrow.
There are times we have been weary of life because we are so full of anxiety.
Because we do not understand others,
we are angry and resentful.
First we try to reason with each other, then we blame.
Every day the suffering increases, making the rift greater.
There are days when we are unwilling to speak to each other,
unwilling to look each other in the face.
And we create internal formations, which last for a long time.
Now we turn to the Three Jewels.
Sincerely recognizing our errors, we bow our heads.** (o)

**We know so well that in our consciousness
are buried all the wholesome seeds,
the seeds of love and understanding and seeds of peace and joy.
But because we do not know how to water them,
the wholesome seeds do not sprout fresh and green.**

We continue to allow sorrow to overwhelm us
until there is no light in our lives.
When we chase after a distant happiness,
life becomes but a shadow of the reality.
Our mind is occupied by the past,
or worrying about this or that in the future.
We cannot let go of our anger,
and we consider of no value the precious gifts of life
which are already in our hands,
thereby trampling on real happiness.
As month follows month, we are sunk in sorrow.
So now in the precious presence of the Buddha,
fragrant with sandalwood incense,
we recognize our errors and begin anew. (o)

With all our heart we go for refuge,
turning to the Buddhas in the Ten Directions
and all the Bodhisattvas, noble disciples, and self-achieved Buddhas.
Very sincerely we recognize our errors
and the mistakes of our wrong judgments.
Please bring the balm of clear water
to pour on the roots of our afflictions.
Please bring the raft of the true teachings
to carry us over the ocean of sorrows.
We vow to live an awakened life,
to practice smiling and conscious breathing,
and to study the teachings, authentically transmitted.

Diligently, we shall live in mindfulness. (o)

We come back to live in the wonderful present,
to plant our heart's garden with good seeds,
and to make strong foundations of understanding and love.
We vow to train ourselves in mindfulness and concentration,
practicing to look and understand deeply
to be able to see the nature of all that is,
and so to be free of the bonds of birth and death.
We learn to speak lovingly, to be affectionate,
to care for others whether it is early morn or late afternoon,
to bring the roots of joy to many places,
helping people to abandon sorrow,
to respond with deep gratitude
to the kindness of parents, teachers, and friends.
With deep faith we light up the incense of our heart.
We ask the Lord of Compassion to be our protector
on the wonderful path of practice.
We vow to practice diligently,
cultivating the fruits of this path. (o)

Namo Shakyamunaye Buddhaya. (3 times) (ooo)

8. CONSECRATION OF WATER

(The leader raises up the bowl of clear water to perform the mudra of peace)

This water's shape is round or square according to the container that holds it.
In the spring warmth, it is liquid; in the winter cold, it is solid.
When its path is open, it flows.
When its path is obstructed, it stands still.
How vast it is, yet its source is so small it is difficult to find.
How wonderful it is in its streams which flow endlessly.
In the jade rivulets, the footprints of dragons remain.
In the deep pond, water holds the bright halo of the autumn moon.
On the tip of the king's pen, water becomes the compassion of clemency.
On the willow branch, it becomes the clear fresh balm of compassion.
Only one drop of the water of compassion is needed, and the Ten Directions are all purified. (o)

The Great Compassion
Avalokiteshvara Bodhisattva. (3 times) (ooo)

9. REFLECTING ON WATER

This water has eight special qualities.
It washes away the dust and impurities of all living beings,
leading them all into the wonderful Avatamsaka World.
May all beings without exception overcome their suffering.
Water does not need to be washed by water, that is the wonderful Dharmakaya.
Dust does not cling to dust, that is how our mind opens naturally.
When we sprinkle the water which is the nectar of compassion,
our place of enlightenment is purified.
The wilting plant grows fresh and green again, the world of defilement changes into a world of purity, and all beings are refreshed and can live in peace and joy.
Homage to the Bodhisattva Who Refreshes the Earth. (o)

The Great Compassion
Avalokiteshvara Bodhisattva. (3 times) (ooo)

- If you have more time, please chant the Amitabha Sutra.

10. CHANTING THE AMITABHA SUTRA

Translated on Imperial Order
by Tripitaka Master Hsuan-tsang of Great T'ang Dynasty translated from Chinese by Hisao Inagaki

[1] MEETING AT JETA GROVE

Thus, have I heard. At one time the Bhagavat was staying in Jeta Grove monastery in Anathapindada's Garden at Shravasti, together with a large company of twelve hundred and fifty monks, who were all venerable shravakas and well-known great arhats. They were headed by eminent shravakas, such as the Venerable Shariputra, Mahamaudgalyayana, Mahakashyapa and Aniruddha. He was also accompanied by innumerable bodhisattvas, mahasattvas, who were all dwelling in the Stage of Non-retrogression and were adorned with immeasurable merits and virtues, headed by great bodhisattvas, such as Bodhisattva Manjushri, Bodhisattva Ajita, Bodhisattva Nityodyukta and Bodhisattva Anikshipta-dhura. Also in the assembly were a hundred thousand kotis of nayutas [of devas] headed by Shakra along with the King of Mahabrahma Heaven, the Lord of Saha world, as well as the Four

Guardian Kings and others. Many demi-gods, innumerable heavenly and human beings, asuras and others assembled and took their seats to hear the Dharma.

[2] INTRODUCTION THE BUDDHA-LANDS

The Bhagavat said to Shariputra: "Do you know that if you travel westwards from here, passing a hundred thousand kotis of nayutas of Buddha-lands, you come to the land called 'Utmost Bliss,' where there is a Bhagavat named 'Amitayus' or 'Amitabha' with ten titles, including Tathagata, Arhat and Samyaksambuddha. He is living there at this very moment, teaching the profound and wonderful Dharma to sentient beings to give them supreme benefit and bliss.

[3] THE SOLEMN PURELAND

Why, Shariputra, is that land called 'Utmost Bliss'? Shariputra, beings in that land suffer no afflictions and pain but experience only pure immeasurable joy and happiness. For this reason, that land is called 'Utmost Bliss.'

Again, Shariputra, in the pure Buddha-land of Utmost Bliss there are seven rows of jewelled balustrades, seven rows of jewelled tala-trees, and sevenfold jewelled nets, which surround

everywhere and are completely decorated with four jewels, namely, gold, silver, beryl and crystal. Shariputra, that Buddha-land is full of such glorious adornments of supreme qualities, which are most pleasing to the mind. For this reason, that land is called 'Utmost Bliss.'

Again, Shariputra, in the pure Buddha-land of Utmost Bliss here and there are many seven-jewelled ponds filled with water of eight excellent qualities, namely, (1) pure, (2) cool, (3) sweet-tasting, (4) soft, (5) moistening, (6) comforting, (7) quenching thirst, hunger and many other needs, and (8) nourishing the senses, increasing the activites of the four elements and producing superior goodness. Sentient beings with a large stock of merits always enjoy using such water. The bottom of these ponds is lined with gold sand, and from the four sides of each pond rise stairs made of the four jewels, most pleasing to the mind. Marvellous jewelled trees surrounding the ponds are evenly spaced, scented with rich fragrance and decorated with the seven delightful jewels, namely, gold, silver, beryl, crystal, rosy pearls, cornelian and sapphire.

In the ponds, at all times, lotuses of various colours as large as chariot-wheels are in bloom. Blue flowers radiate blue light, brilliance and splendor; yellow ones radiate yellow light,

brilliance and splendor; red ones radiate red light, brilliance and splendour; white ones radiate white light, brilliance and splendor; four-coloured ones radiate four-coloured light, brilliance and splendor. Shariputra, that Buddha-land is full of such glorious adornments of supreme qualities, which are most pleasing to the mind. For this reason, that land is called 'Utmost Bliss.'

Again, Shariputra, in that pure Buddha-land of Utmost Bliss limitless exquisite music is spontaneously played at all times. The sound is harmonious and most pleasant to hear. When sentient beings hear its excellent sound, their evil passions are completely removed, numerous good acts multiply, and they soon attain the highest perfect Enlightenment. Shariputra, that Buddha-land is full of such glorious adornments of supreme qualities, which are most pleasing to the mind. For this reason, that land is called 'Utmost Bliss.'

Again, Shariputra, the ground throughout that pure Buddha-land of Utmost Bliss is of true gold. It is soft to the touch and refreshing, shining boundlessly and adorned with rare jewels. Shariputra, that Buddha-land is full of such glorious adornments of supreme qualities, which are most pleasing to the mind. For this reason,

that land is called 'Utmost Bliss.'

Again, Shariputra, in that pure Buddha-land of Utmost Bliss, six times during the day and night, various heavenly blossoms of rare beauty continuously rain down from the sky. They are brilliant and refreshing, soft and variegated, pleasing to the mind and the senses. They do not rouse greedy attachment, but increase countless inconceivable merits in sentient beings. Six times during the day and night, the beings in that land offer those blossoms to Amitayus in homage. Every morning they take those heavenly blossoms and, in such a short time it takes for a meal, fly to innumerable other lands to pay homage to a hundred, thousand kotis of Buddhas. They offer to each Buddha a hundred thousand kotis of such blossoms and return home to the Pure Land, as if to enjoy leisure in a heavenly abode. Shariputra, that Buddha-land is full of such glorious adornments of supreme qualities, which are most pleasing to the mind. For this reason, that land is called 'Utmost Bliss.'

Again, Shariputra, in that pure Buddha-land of Utmost Bliss there are always many rare species of beautiful birds of various colours, such as swams, geese, herons, storks, cranes, peacocks, parrots, kalavinkas and jivamjivakas. Six times during the day and night, those birds form a

flock and sing with melodious and delicate tones, producing diverse sounds to proclaim numerous wonderful teachings, such as the [four] mindful acts, the [four] ways of stopping evils, the [four] miraculous powers, the [five] roots of goodness, the [five] powers, the [seven] factors of wisdom, and the [Eightfold] Noble Path. Having heard their singing, the sentient beings in that land gain innumerable merits through mindfulness of the Buddha, Dharma and Sangha, and their bodies long retain the perfume of virtue. Shariputra, do you think that the birds in that land belong to the evil realm of animals? Do not hold such a view! The reason is that none of the three evil realms, not even their names, exist in that Buddha's Pure Land; how much less should there be real birds belonging to the realm of animals born as retribution for evil karma? You should know that they are manifestations created by Amitayus so that they can proclaim innumerable sounds of the Dharma to give benefit and bliss to sentient beings. Shariputra, that Buddha-land is full of such wonderful glorious adornments, which are most pleasing to the mind. For this reason, that land is called 'Utmost Bliss.'

Again, Shariputra, in that pure Buddha-land of Utmost Bliss soft breezes always blow. When they waft through the jewelled trees and jewelled nets,

wonderful sounds are produced. As if a hundred thousand kotis of celestial musical instruments were playing together to produce exquisite sounds, when soft breezes which constantly arise in that land waft through the jewelled trees and jewelled nets, they produce various excellent sounds, which proclaim many teachings of the Dharma. Having heard those sounds, sentient beings in that land give rise to numerous meritorious acts, such as mindfulness of the Buddha, Dharma and Sangha. Shariputra, that Buddha-land is full of such glorious adornments of supreme qualities, which are most pleasing to the mind. For this reason, that land is called 'Utmost Bliss.'

Shariputra, in that pure Buddha-land of Utmost Bliss there are wonderful manifestations such as those, which are innumerable and inconceivable. Even if a hundred thousand kotis of nayutas of innumerable tongues should praise their excellent qualities for a hundred thousand kotis of nayutas of kalpas, each tongue producing immeasurable voices, they would not be able to praise them to the full. For this reason, [that land] is called the Land of Utmost Bliss.

[4] INTRODUCTION THE AMITABHA BUDDHA

Again, Shariputra, why is the Buddha of the pure Buddha-land of Utmost Bliss called 'Amitayus'? Because, Shariputra, the life-span of that Tathagata and all beings living there last for immeasurable and innumerable great kalpas, the Tathagata of that land is called 'Amitayus.' Shariputra, why is the Buddha also called 'Amitabha'? Shariputra, the Tathagata always emits boundless and innumerable rays of glorious light, illuminating all the Buddha-lands of the ten directions without hindrance, so as to display Buddhist activities. For this reason, the Tathagata of that land is called 'Amitabha.' Shariputra, the Pure Land of that Buddha is full of such glorious adornments, which are most pleasing to the mind. For this reason, that land is called 'Utmost Bliss.'

Again, Shariputra, the Buddha Amitayus of that pure Buddha-land of Utmost Bliss always has shravaka disciples, all of them arhats, who are possessed of various excellent merits and whose number is unlimited and incalculable. Shariputra, the Pure Land of that Buddha is full of such glorious adornments, which are most pleasing to the mind. For this reason, that land is called 'Utmost Bliss.'

Again, Shariputra, the Buddha Amitayus of that pure Buddha-land of Utmost Bliss always has innumerable bodhisattva disciples, all of them in the Stage of Becoming a Buddha after One More Life. They are possessed of various excellent merits, and their number is unlimited and incalculable. Even if one praised their merits for innumerable kalpas, one would not be able to praise them fully. Shariputra, that Buddha-land is filled with such glorious adornments, which are most pleasing to the mind. For this reason, that land is called 'Utmost Bliss.'

[5] THE GREAT CAUSE TO BE BORN IN THE UTMOST BLISSFUL LAND

Again, Shariputra, sentient beings born in that land all dwell in the Stage of Non-retrogression, and will not fall again into an evil realm, be born in a border-land or in the state of debased people or mlecchas. They always enjoy visiting pure lands of other Buddhas. With their excellent vows and practice advancing and developing every moment, they will unfailingly realize the highest, perfect Enlightenment. Shariputra, that Buddha-land is full of such glorious merits, which are most pleasing to the mind. For this reason, that land is called 'Utmost Bliss.'

Again, Shariputra, if sentient beings hear of

the glorious manifestations of countless merits in that pure Buddha-land of Amitayus, they should all awaken aspiration to be born there. The reasons are: first, those born there will meet those Great Beings adorned with such countless merits as mentioned above; second, they will enjoy the pleasure of the Mahayana Dharma intrinsic to this pure Buddha-land adorned with such innumerable merits; and third, with their own immeasurable vows and practice advancing and developing every moment, they will quickly realize the highest perfect Enlightenment. Shariputra, those who are to be born in that Buddha-land do not have few but already countless and unlimited merits, so such sentient beings can attain birth in the pure Buddha-land of Utmost Bliss of the Buddha Amitayus.

Again, Shariputra, if good men or women of pure faith, having heard Amitayus Buddha's name of innumerable, boundless and inconceivable merits and also heard of the glorious adornments of the Land of Utmost Bliss, concentrate their thoughts on them with undistracted mind even for one day, two days, three, four, five, six or seven days, then, at the hour of death, Amitayus, surrounded by innumerable shravaka disciples and bodhisattvas, will appear before those good men or women and give them compassionate

protection to keep their minds from falling into confusion. Thus, after death, following the Buddha Amitayus and his retinue, they will be born in his Pure Land of Utmost Bliss.

Shariputra, as I perceive that such blissful benefits are matters of great importance, I pronounce these words of truth: Good men and good women of pure faith who hear Amitayus Buddha's name of inconceivable merits and also learn of the pure Buddha-land of Utmost Bliss should all receive [the teaching] in faith, arouse aspiration, practise the method as prescribed, and attain birth in that Buddha-land.

[6] SIX DIRECTIONS ALL PRAISED THE BUDDHA LANDS

Shariputra, just as I praise the innumerable, unlimited and inconceivable merits of the Buddha-land of Amitayus, so do the Buddhas of the eastern direction as numerous as the sands of the Ganges, such as Aksobhya Tathagata, Meru-dhvaja Tathagata, Mahameru Tathagata, Meru-prabhasa Tathagata, and Manju-dhvaja Tathagata. While dwelling in their own pure lands of the east, they extend their long, broad tongues and, encompassing with them the universe of a thousand million worlds, pronounce these words of truth: Sentient beings should all receive in

faith this gate of the Dharma concerning praise of the inconceivable merits of the Buddha-land and protection by all Buddhas.

[7] THE SOUTH

Again, Shariputra, there are in the southern direction Buddhas as numerous as the sands of the Ganges, such as Candra-surya-pradipa Tathagata, Yashah-prabha Tathagata, Maharci-skandha Tathagata, Meru-pradipa Tathagata and Ananta-virya Tathagata. While dwelling in their own pure lands of the south, they extend their long, broad tongues and, encompassing with them the universe of a thousand million worlds, pronounce these words of truth: Sentient beings should all receive in faith this gate of the Dharma concerning praise of the inconceivable merits of the Buddha-land and protection by all Buddhas.

[8] THE WEST

Again, Shariputra, there are in the western direction Buddhas as numerous as the sands of the Ganges, such as Amitayus Tathagata, Amita-skandha Tathagata, Amita-prabha Tathagata, Amita-dhvaja Tathagata, Maheshvara Tathagata, Mahaprabha Tathagata, Jvalana

Tathagata, Maharatna-ketu Tathagata and Sphuta-rashmi Tathagata. While dwelling in their own pure lands of the west, they extend their long, broad tongues and, encompassing with them the universe of a thousand million worlds, pronounce these words of truth: Sentient beings should all receive in faith this gate of the Dharma concerning praise of the inconceivable merits of the Buddha-land and protection by all Buddhas.

[9] THE NORTH

Again, Shariputra, there are in the northern direction Buddhas as numerous as the sands of the Ganges, such as Amita-prabha-vyuha-abhijna- buddhi Tathagata, Mahaskandha Tathagata, Amita-divya-dundubhi-vaishvanara-nirghosa Tathagata, Jaleni-prabha Tathagata and Salendra-raja Tathagata. While dwelling in their own pure lands of the north, they extend their long, broad tongues and, encompassing with them the universe of a thousand million worlds, pronounce these words of truth: Sentient beings should all receive in faith this gate of the Dharma concerning praise of the inconceivable merits of the Buddha-land and protection by all Buddhas.

[10] THE NADIR

Again, Shariputra, there are in the nadir Buddhas as numerous as the sands of the Ganges, such as Sarva-saddharma-darshana-yukti-sada-jvalana- rajottama-shri-prabha Tathagata, Simha Tathagata, Yashas Tathagata, Yashah-prabhasa Tathagata, Dharma Tathagata, Saddharma Tathagata, Dharma-dhvaja Tathagata, Guna-mitra Tathagata and Guna-nama Tathagata. While dwelling in their own pure lands of the nadir, they extend their long, broad tongues and, encompassing with them the universe of a thousand million worlds, pronounce these words of truth: Sentient beings should all receive in faith this Dharma-gate expounding praise of the inconceivable merits of the Buddha-land and protection by all Buddhas.

[11] THE ZENITH

Again, Shariputra, there are in the zenith Buddhas as numerous as the sands of the Ganges, such as Brahma-ghosa Tathagata, Naksatra-raja Tathagata, Gandha-prabhasa Tathagata, Utpala-shri-kalpa Tathagata and Sarvartha-darsha Tathagata. While dwelling in their own pure lands of the zenith, they extend their long, broad tongues and, encompassing with them the universe of a thousand million worlds,

pronounce these words of truth: Sentient beings should all receive in faith this gate of the Dharma concerning praise of the inconceivable merits of the Buddha-land and protection by all Buddhas.

[12] THE SOUTH-EASTERN

Again, Shariputra, there are in the south-eastern direction Buddhas as numerous as the sands of the Ganges, such as Uttama-vipula-megha-ghosa-raja Tathagata. While dwelling in their own pure lands of the south-east, they extend their long, broad tongues and, encompassing with them the universe of a thousand million worlds, pronounce these words of truth: Sentient beings should all receive in faith this gate of the Dharma concerning praise of the inconceivable merits of the Buddha-land and protection by all Buddhas.

[13] THE SOUTH-WESTERN

Again, Shariputra, there are in the south-western direction Buddhas as numerous as the sands of the Ganges, such as Uttama-surya-prabha-yasho-guna Tathagata. While dwelling in their own pure lands of the south-west, they extend their long, broad tongues and, encompassing with them the universe of a thousand million

worlds, pronounce these words of truth: Sentient beings should all receive in faith this gate of the Dharma concerning praise of the inconceivable merits of the Buddha-land and protection by all Buddhas.

[14] THE NORTH-WESTERN

Again, Shariputra, there are in the north-western direction Buddhas as numerous as the sands of the Ganges, such as Amita-guna-jvalanadhipati-prabhasa Tathagata. While dwelling in their own pure lands of the north-west, they extend their long, broad tongues and, encompassing with them the universe of a thousand million worlds, pronounce these words of truth: Sentient beings should all receive in faith this gate of the Dharma concerning praise of the inconceivable merits of the Buddha-land and protection by all Buddhas.

[15] THE NORTH-EASTERN

Again, Shariputra, there are in the north-eastern direction Buddhas as numerous as the sands of the Ganges, such as Asamkhya-shata-sahasra-koti- nayuta-vipula-buddhi Tathagata. While dwelling in their own pure lands of the north-east, they extend their long, broad tongues and, encompassing with them the universe of a

thousand million worlds, pronounce these words of truth: Sentient beings should all receive in faith this gate of the Dharma concerning praise of the inconceivable merits of the Buddha-land and protection by all Buddhas.

[16] THE INCONCEIVABLE MERIT OF THE AMITABHA SUTRA

Shariputra, why is this sutra named 'the Dharma-gate expounding praise of the inconceivable merits of the Buddha-land and protection by all Buddhas? Shariputra, it is revealed in this sutra that the inconceivable merits of Amitayus Buddha's Land of Utmost Bliss are praised and glorified and that all Buddhas, Bhagavats, of the ten directions, while dwelling in their own lands, display glorious and wonderful manifestations and pronounce words of truth, urging sentient beings to receive this teaching in faith, in order to guide and benefit them and give them peace and bliss. For this reason, this sutra is called 'the gate of the Dharma concerning praise of the inconceivable merits of the Buddha-land and protection by all Buddhas.'

Shariputra, if good men or women, who have heard this sutra, now hear or will hear it, have already awakened or will awaken deep faith, they are embraced by those Buddhas, Bhagavats,

dwelling in the ten directions, as numerous as ten times the number of the sands of the Ganges. All who practise as prescribed will not regress but will definitely attain the highest perfect Enlightenment and be born in the Pure Land of Utmost Bliss of Amitayus. For this reason, Shariputra, all sentient beings should receive in faith and understand well my words and the words of the Buddhas, Bhagavats, of the ten directions, and should make great efforts and diligently practise as prescribed. Do not allow any doubt to arise.

Again, Shariputra, if good men or women have already aspired or will aspire or now aspire to the glorious adornments in the Pure Land of Utmost Bliss of Amitayus, they will be definitely embraced by those Buddhas, Bhagavats, dwelling in the ten directions, as numerous as the sands of the Ganges, even ten times that number. All who practise as prescribed will not regress but will definitely attain the highest perfect Enlightenment and be born in the Pure Land of Utmost Bliss of Amitayus. For this reason, Shariputra, good men and women of pure faith should all believe deeply in Amitayus Buddha's Pure Land of Utmost Bliss and aspire to be born there. Do not be indolent.

[17] THE AMITABHA SUTRA IS THE MOST DIFFICULT FOR THE WORLD TO ACCEPT

Shariputra, just as I now praise and glorify the inconceivable merits of Amitayus Buddha's Land of Utmost Bliss, all other Buddhas, Bhagavats, of the ten directions likewise praise my boundless inconceivable merits, saying: 'How marvellous it is that Shakyamuni, Shakya Dharma-King, Tathagata, Arthat, Samyaksambuddha, Possessed of Wisdom and Practice, Sugata, Knower of the World, the Unsurpassed, Tamer of Men, Teacher of Gods and Humans, Buddha and Bhagavat, has appeared in this Saha world during the period of the five corruptions: namely, those of time, sentient beings, passions, views and life-span, and that, having attained the highest perfect Enlightenment, delivered this teaching, most difficult for the world to accept, in order to guide and benefit sentient beings and give them peace and bliss.'

Thus, Shariputra, you should know that I have appeared in this Saha world of various defilements during the period of the five corruptions and, having attained the highest perfect Enlightenment, delivered this teaching, most difficult for the world to accept, in order to guide and benefit sentient beings and give them peace and bliss. This is indeed a rare and

marvellous task, which is beyond comprehension. "If, Shariputra, there are good men or women of pure faith who, having heard this teaching, most difficult for the world to accept, receive it in faith, uphold and expound it to others, and practise it as prescribed, you should know that such people are extremely rare. In the past they have planted roots of goodness in the presence of innumerable Buddhas. After death they will surely be born in the Western Land of Utmost Bliss, where they will enjoy various glorious adornments and the pleasure of Mahayana Dharma embodied in the Buddha's Pure Land. They can approach Amitayus Buddha and make offerings to him six times during the day and night. They can also fly to [the lands in] the ten directions to make offerings to Buddhas, where they will hear the Dharma taught by them and will receive assurances of their attainment of Buddhahood. Thus they will be able to perfect quickly the merits and wisdom and realize the highest perfect Enlightenment."

[18] SUPPORTED BY INNUMERABLE DEVAS, HUMANS, ASURAS & THE DHARMA PROTECTIVE DEITIES

When the Bhavagat had delivered this sutra, all the great shravakas, such as the Venerable

Shariputra, and bodhisattvas, mahasattvas, together with all beings, including innumerable devas, humans and asuras, greatly rejoiced at the Buddha's exposition and received it in faith.

11. THE INSIGHT THAT BRINGS US TO THE OTHER SHORE

The Heart of Prajnaparamita (Perfect Wisdom)

Avalokiteshvara while practicing deeply with the Insight that Brings Us to the Other Shore, suddenly discovered that all of the five Skandhas are equally empty, and with this realization he overcame all Ill-being (suffering). (o)

Listen Sariputra, this Body itself is Emptiness and Emptiness itself is this Body.

This Body is not other than Emptiness and Emptiness is not other than this Body.

The same is true of Feelings, Perceptions, Mental Formations, and Consciousness. (o)

Listen Sariputra, all phenomena bear the mark of Emptiness; their true nature is the nature of neither Birth nor Death, neither

Being nor Non-being, neither Defilement nor Purity, neither Increasing nor Decreasing. (o)

That is why in Emptiness, Body, Feelings, Perceptions, Mental Formations and Consciousness are not separate self-entities. The Eighteen Realms of Phenomena which are the six Sense Organs, six Sense Objects, and six Consciousnesses are also not separate self-entities. (o)

The Twelve Links of Interdependent Arising and their Extinction are also not separate self-entities. Ill-being, the Causes of Ill-being, the End of Ill-being, the Path, insight and attainment, are also not separate self-entities. Whoever can see this no longer needs anything to attain. (o)

Bodhisattvas who practice the Insight that Brings Us to the Other Shore see no more obstacles in their mind, and because there are no more obstacles in their mind, they can overcome all fear, destroy all wrong perceptions and realize Perfect Nirvana.

All Buddhas in the past, present and future by practicing the Insight that Brings Us to the Other Shore, are all capable of attaining Authentic and

Perfect Enlightenment. (o)

Therefore, Sariputra, it should be known that the Insight that Brings Us to the Other Shore is a Great Mantra, the most illuminating mantra, the highest mantra, a mantra beyond compare, the True Wisdom that has the power to put an end to all kinds of suffering. (o)

Therefore, let us proclaim a mantra. To praise the Insight that Brings Us to the Other Shore. Gone, gone, gone beyond, gone to the other shore, awake, rejoice! (3 times) (o)

Namo the Great Compassionate

Avalokiteshvara Bodhisattva. (3 times) (ooo)

12. READ THE NAMES OF THE BUDDHAS AND BODHISATTVAS

The river of attachment is ten thousand miles long.

The waves on the ocean of confusion stretch so far.

If you wish to go beyond the realms of samsara,

Recollect the Buddha with one pointed mind. (o)

The Pure Land is available in our True Mind.

Amitabha manifests from the true nature of things,

Shining light on the three worlds and the ten directions,

Always abiding in the present moment.

May I go back to Amitabha Buddha,

The founder of the Pure Land,

The source of limitless lifespan.

May I with one heart visualize and recollect this holy name.

Namo Amitabhaya Buddhaya, the Buddha of Infinite Light. (3 times) (o)

Namo Manjushri, the Bodhisattva of Great Understanding. (3 times) (o)

Namo Samantabhadra, the Bodhisattva of Great Action. (3 times) (o)

Namo Avalokiteshvara, the Bodhisattva of Great Compassion. (3 times) (o)

Namo Kshitigarbhaya Bodhisattvaya,
the Bodhisattva of Great Aspiration.
(3 times) (ooo)

13. TAKING REFUGE IN AMITABHA BUDDHA

Taking refuge in the Amitabha Buddha

In the wondrous ultimate dimension,
I devote my heart to returning to myself
And holding to the source of mindfulness.
I have vowed to go for refuge to the Amitabha Buddha. (o)

I bow my head and ask the Buddha
To receive us in his embrace.
As the Pure Land manifests,
Please bring your torch of light
To shine onto my thoughts.
Please bring the boat of long lifespan
To carry my body through life
So I live with peace and joy,
So my aspiration can be fully realized.
Buddha, please always protect me. (o)

Not letting my mind grow slack,
So that I end wrong perceptions
And the affliction fall away.
In the present moment
Buddha can be found in this world.
Taking every step with solidity and freedom

We walk in the Pure Land.
When we live the present moment mindfully,
The Pure Land is already a reality.
So whatever form we take in the future,
We can be assured of peace and joy. (o)

If we are able to recollect the Amitabha
With undispersed, one-pointed mind,
The nine lotus grades will appear.
May we enjoy life for ourselves and others
And know in advance our time of death.
At death may our mind not flinch,
Our body not be sick and in pain,
Our thoughts not waiver. (o)

May the Amitabha and his holy assembly
Holding up the golden lotuses
Be present without delay.
Together may we set out in freedom
May we see the Buddha in the opening lotus.
May the Pure Land be our home.
I bow my head to ask Buddha to be my witness
To my never slackening practice. (o)

Namo Amitabha Buddha. (3 times) (ooo)

14. MAY THE DAY & NIGHT BE WELL

May the day be well and the night be well.
May the midday hour bring happiness too.
In every minute and every second, may the day and night be well.
By the blessing of the Triple Gem, may all things be protected and safe.
May all beings born in each of the four ways live in a land of purity.
May all in the Three Realms be born upon Lotus Thrones.
May countless wandering souls realize the three virtuous positions of the Bodhisattva Path.
May all living beings, with grace and ease, fulfill the Bodhisattva Stages.
The countenance of the World-Honored One, like the full moon
or like the orb of the sun, shines with the light of clarity.
A halo of wisdom spreads in every direction, enveloping all with love and compassion, joy and equanimity.

Namo Shakyamunaye Buddhaya. (3 times) (ooo)

15. THINK OF THE DECEASED

Dear all Families and Relatives of the Deceased,

It is time to bring to mind to the deceased (the full name, the Dharma name, longevity…) **and to send the energy of loving kindness and compassion to him/her. Let us sit and enjoy our present for a moment, allowing the deceased to be present with us now.**

The peace and joy of the entire world, including the worlds of the living and the dead, depend upon our own peace and joy in this moment. With all our heart and one-pointed mind, let us begin anew for the benefit of ourselves and our beloved ones.

May the deceased be peaceful at the new form. (o)

Namo Amitabha Buddhaya. (ooo)

16. GATHA ON IMPERMANENCE

The day is now ended. Our lives are shorter.

Let us look carefully. What have we done?

Noble Sangha, with all our heart,

let us be diligent, engaging in the practice.

Let us live deeply, free from our afflictions,

aware of impermanence so that life does not drift away without meaning. (ooo)

17.PRAYER FOR THE DECEASED

Namo Amitabha Buddhaya. (o)

Namo the Buddhas, Bodhisattvas and the Dharma Protective Deities prove,

Today, on the ceremony of of blessing for the deceased, entering coffin/ closing coffin/ moving coffin/ cremation/ bury, the Seventh/ Forty-ninth Days or the dead anniversary… of the deceased the dead anniversary… of the deceased, we are… (the leader Bhikkhuni…) **with the sangha members at..., chanted the...... Sutra, meditated, read the Amitabha Buddha's name and practiced the meritorious deeds.** (o)

We would like to Return this merit to pray for the deceased... (the full name, the Dharma name, longevity…) **with our ancestors and parents in the past, the heroic warriors sacrificed for the country, the deceased died in rivers, accidents and other reasons. There are twelve kinds of souls with names or unname. May all of them overcome the suffering ocean of the bad karma and be peaceful at the Pure land and practice with Buddhas and Bodhisattvas.**

Again, we give back this merit to pray for Buddhists... (the full name, the Dharma name, age…) **together with the householders and all Sangha members present here are always healthy, happy and diligent in practice. May all year round be auspicious and joy. May our bodhicitta firm; our wills are steady; and we will gain self-awareness as well as the perfective enlightenment.** (o)

Finally, may all sentient beings soon complete the Way of Love and Understanding.

Namo Amitabha Buddhaya. (ooo)

18. SALUTATION THOUSANDS BUDDHAS IN THREE TIMES

There are many the great causes

The ten directions, three lives and realms

The deceased keeps his/her body and mind pure

Pay homage at all without being left behind. (o)

On behalf of the deceased, we pay respects sincerely to the four graces of the three realms:

Namo the Buddhas of the kalpa thousands in the past. (o) (1 prostration)

Namo the Buddhas of the kalpa thousands in the present. (o) (1 prostration)

Namo the Buddhas of the kalpa thousands in the future. (ooo) (1 prostration)

19.THE REFUGE CHANT

Incense perfumes the atmosphere.

A lotus blooms and the Buddha appears. The world of suffering and discrimination is filled with the light of the rising sun.

As the dust of fear and anxiety settles, with open heart, one-pointed mind, the deceased turns to the Three Jewels. (o)

The Fully Enlightened One, beautifully seated, peaceful and smiling, a living source of understanding and compassion, to the Buddha, the deceased goes for refuge. (o)

The path of mindful living, leading to healing, joy, and enlightenment, the way of peace, to the Dharma, the deceased goes for refuge. (o)

The loving and supportive community of practice, realizing harmony, awareness, and liberation, to the Sangha, the deceased goes for refuge. (o)

The deceased is aware that the Three Gems are

within his/her heart.

The deceased vows to realize them, practicing mindful breathing and smiling, looking deeply into things.

The deceased vows to understand living beings and their suffering, to cultivate compassion and loving kindness, to practice joy and equanimity. (o)

The deceased vows to offer joy to one person in the morning, to help relieve the grief of one person in the afternoon, living simply and sanely with few possessions, keeping his/her body healthy.

The deceased vows to let go of all worries and anxiety in order to be light and free. (o)

The deceased is aware that he/she owes so much to his/her parents, teachers, friends, and all beings.

The deceased vows to be worthy of their trust, to practice wholeheartedly so that understanding and compassion will flower, helping living beings be free from their suffering.

May the Buddha, the Dharma, and the Sangha support his/her efforts. (ooo)

20. TAKING REFUGE AT THREE JEWELS

-I take refuge in the Buddha,

the one who shows me the way in this life.

I take refuge in the Dharma,

the way of understanding and of love.

I take refuge in the Sangha,

the community that lives in harmony and awareness. (o) (1 prostration)

-Dwelling in the refuge of Buddha,

I clearly see the path of light and beauty in the world.

Dwelling in the refuge of Dharma,

I learn to open many doors on the path of transformation.

Dwelling in the refuge of Sangha,

shining light that supports me, keeping my practice free of obstruction. (o) (1 prostration)

-Taking refuge in the Buddha in myself,

I aspire to help all people recognize their own awakened nature,

realizing the Mind of Love.

Taking refuge in the Dharma in myself,

I aspire to help all people fully master the ways of practice

and walk together on the path of liberation.

Taking refuge in the Sangha in myself,

I aspire to help all people build Fourfold Communities,

to embrace all beings and support their transformation. (ooo) (1 prostration)

21. SHARING THE MERIT & VERSE FOR CLOSING

Reciting the sutras, practicing the way of awareness gives rise to benefits without limit.

We vow to share the fruits with all beings.

We vow to offer tribute to parents, teachers, friends, and numerous beings who give guidance and support along the path. (o)

May we be born now in the Pure Land within the heart of a lotus flower.

In the moment when the lotus blooms, we touch the reality of no-birth and no-dying.

May Buddhas and Bodhisattvas be our companions on the wonderful path of practice. (o)

May we end all afflictions so that understanding can arise, the obstacles of unwholesome acts be dissolved, and the fruit of awakening be fully realized. (o)

Namo Amitabha Buddhaya. (3 times) (ooo)

22. WORDS OF GRATITUDE

A family member, relative or friend of the deceased is invited to come mindfully before the community to speak about the virtues and achievements of the deceased and to offer a few words of gratitude to sangha and visitors who participated in the ceremony.

BẢO ANH LẠC BOOKSHELF

Dr. Bhikṣuṇī TN Giới Hương composed

A. THE VIETNAMESE BOOKS

1. *Bồ-tát và Tánh Không Trong Kinh Tạng Pali và Đại Thừa* (Boddhisattva and Sunyata in the Early and Developed Buddhist Traditions).
2. *Ban Mai Xứ Ấn* (The Dawn in India), (3 tập).
3. *Vườn Nai – Chiếc Nôi* (Phật Giáo Deer Park–The Cradle of Buddhism).
4. *Quy Y Tam Bảo và Năm Giới* (Take Refuge in Three Gems and Keep the Five Precepts).
5. *Vòng Luân Hồi* (The Cycle of Life).
6. *Hoa Tuyết Milwaukee* (Snowflake in Milwaukee).
7. *Luân Hồi trong Lăng Kính Lăng Nghiêm* (The Rebirth in *Śūrangama* Sūtra).
8. *Nghi Thức Hộ Niệm, Cầu Siêu* (The Ritual for the Deceased).
9. *Quan Âm Quảng Trần* (The Commentary of Avalokiteśvara Bodhisattva).
10. *Nữ Tu và Tù Nhân Hoa Kỳ* (A Nun and American Inmates).
11. *Nếp Sống Tỉnh Thức của Đức Đạt Lai Lạt Ma Thứ XIV* (The Awakened Mind of the 14th Dalai Lama).
12. *A-Hàm: Mưa pháp chuyển hóa phiền não* (*Agama – A Dharma Rain transforms the Defilement*), 2 tập.
13. *Góp Từng Hạt Nắng Perris* (Collection of Sunlight in

Perris).

14. *Pháp Ngữ của Kinh Kim Cang* (The Key Words of Vajracchedikā-Prajñāpāramitā-Sūtra).
15. *Tập Thơ Nhạc Nắng Lăng Nghiêm* (Songs and Poems of Śūraṅgama Sunlight).
16. *Nét Bút Bên Song Cửa* (Reflections at the Temple Window).
17. *Máy Nghe MP3 Hương Sen* (Hương Sen Digital Mp3 Radio Speaker): Các Bài Giảng, Sách, Bài viết và Thơ Nhạc của Thích Nữ Giới Hương (383/201 bài).
18. *DVD Giới Thiệu về Chùa Hương Sen*, USA (Introduction on Huong Sen Temple).
19. *Ni Giới Việt Nam Hoằng Pháp tại Hoa Kỳ* (Sharing the Dharma - Vietnamese Buddhist Nuns in the United States).
20. *Tuyển Tập 40 Năm Tu Học & Hoằng Pháp của Ni sư Giới Hương* (Forty Years in the Dharma: A Life of Study and Service—Venerable Bhikkhuni Giới Hương), Thích Nữ Viên Quang, TN Viên Nhuận, TN Viên Tiến, and TN Viên Khuông.
21. *Tập Thơ Nhạc Lối Về Sen Nở (Songs and Poems of Lotus Blooming on the Way).*
22. *Nghi Thức Công Phu Khuya – Thần Chú Thủ Lăng Nghiêm* (Śūraṅgama Mantra).
23. *Nghi Thức Cầu An – Kinh Phổ Môn* (The Universal Door Sūtra).
24. *Nghi Thức Cầu An – Kinh Dược Sư* (The Medicine Buddha Sūtra).

25. *Nghi Thức Sám Hối Hồng Danh* (The Sūtra of Confession at many Buddha Titles).
26. *Nghi Thức Công Phu Chiều – Mông Sơn Thí Thực* (The Ritual Donating Food to Hungry Ghosts).
27. *Khóa Tịnh Độ – Kinh A Di Đà* (The Amitabha Buddha Sūtra).
28. *Nghi Thức Cúng Linh và Cầu Siêu* (The Rite for Deceased and Funeral Home).
29. *Nghi Lễ Hàng Ngày - 50 Kinh Tụng và các Lễ Vía trong Năm* (The Daily Chanting Rituals and Annual Ceremonies).
30. *Hương Đạo Trong Đời 2022* (Tuyển tập 60 Bài Thi trong Cuộc Thi Viết Văn Ứng Dụng Phật Pháp 2022 - A Collection of Writings on the Practicing of Buddhism in Daily Life in the Writing Contest 2022).
31. *Hương Pháp 2022* (Tuyển Tập Các Bài Thi Trúng Giải Cuộc Thi Viết Văn Ứng Dụng Phật Pháp 2022 - A Collection of the Winning Writings on the Practicing of Buddhism in Daily Life in the Writing Contest 2022).
32. *Giới Hương - Thơm Ngược Gió Ngàn*, Nguyên Hà.
33. *Pháp Ngữ Kinh Hoa Nghiêm* (2 tập). Thích Nữ Giới Hương.
34. *Tinh Hoa Kinh Hoa Nghiêm*. Thích Nữ Giới Hương. NXB Hương Sen.
35. *Phật Giáo và Đại Dịch Coronavirus Covid-19*. Thích Nữ Giới Hương.
36. *Phật Giáo – Tầm Nhìn Lịch Sử Và Thực Hành.* Hiệu đính: Thích Hạnh Chánh và Thích Nữ Giới Hương.

B. THE ENGLISH BOOKS

1. Boddhisattva and Sunyata in the Early and Developed Buddhist Traditions.
2. *Rebirth Views in the Śūraṅgama Sūtra.*
3. *Commentary of Avalokiteśvara Bodhisattva.*
4. *The Key Words in Vajracchedikā Sūtra.*
5. *Sārnātha-The Cradle of Buddhism in the Archeological View.*
6. *Take Refuge in the Three Gems and Keep the Five Precepts.*
7. *Cycle of Life.*
8. *Forty Years in the Dharma: A Life of Study and Service—Venerable Bhikkhuni Giới Hương.*
9. *Sharing the Dharma -Vietnamese Buddhist Nuns in the United States.*
10. *A Vietnamese Buddhist Nun and American Inmates.*
11. *Daily Monastic Chanting.*
12. *Weekly Buddhist Discourse Chanting.*
13. *Practice Meditation and Pure Land.*
14. *The Ceremony for Peace.*
15. *The Lunch Offering Ritual.*
16. *The Ritual Offering Food to Hungry Ghosts.*
17. *The Pureland Course of Amitabha Sutra.*
18. *The Medicine Buddha Sutra.*
19. *The New Year Ceremony.*
20. *The Great Parinirvana Ceremony.*

21. *The Buddha's Birthday Ceremony.*
22. *The Ullambana Festival (Parents' Day).*
23. *The Marriage Ceremony.*
24. *The Blessing Ceremony for The Deceased.*
25. *The Ceremony Praising Ancestral Masters.*
26. *The Enlightened Buddha Ceremony.*
27. *The Uposatha Ceremony (Reciting Precepts).*
28. *Buddhism: A Historical and Practical Vision.* Edited by Ven. Dr. Thich Hanh Chanh and Ven. Dr. Bhikṣuṇī TN Gioi Huong.
29. *Contribution of Buddhism For World Peace & Social Harmony*. Edited by Ven. Dr. Buddha Priya Mahathero and Ven. Dr. Bhikṣuṇī TN Gioi Huong.
30. *Global Spread of Buddhism with Special Reference to Sri Lanka*. Buddhist Studies Seminar in Kandy University. Edited by Dr. Ven. Kahawatte Siri Sumedha Thero and Dr. Bhikṣuṇī TN Gioi Huong.
31. *Buddhism In Sri Lanka During The Period of 19th to 21st Centuries*. Buddhist Studies Seminar in Colombo. Edited by Prof. Ven. Medagama Nandawansa and Dr. Bhikṣuṇī TN Gioi Huong.

C. THE BILINGUAL BOOKS (VIETNAMESE-ENGLISH)

1. *Bản Tin Hương Sen: Xuân, Phật Đản, Vu Lan (*Hương Sen Newsletter: Spring, Buddha Birthday and Vu Lan, annual/ Mỗi Năm).
2. *Danh Ngôn Nuôi Dưỡng Nhân Cách - Good Sentences*

Nurture a Good Manner.

3. *Văn Hóa Đặc Sắc của Nước Nhật Bản-Exploring the Unique Culture of Japan.*
4. *Sống An Lạc dù Đời không Đẹp như Mơ - Live Peacefully though Life is not Beautiful as a Dream.*
5. *Hãy Nói Lời Yêu Thương-Words of Love and Understanding.*
6. *Văn Hóa Cổ Kim qua Hành Hương Chiêm Bái -The Ancient- Present Culture in Pilgrim.*
7. *Nghệ Thuật Biết Sống - Art of Living.*

D. THE TRANSLATED BOOKS

1. *Xá Lợi Của Đức Phật* (Relics of the Buddha), Tham Weng Yew.
2. *Sen Nở Nơi Chốn Tử Tù* (Lotus in Prison), many authors.
3. *Chùa Việt Nam Hải Ngoại* (Overseas Vietnamese Buddhist Temples).
4. *Việt Nam Danh Lam Cổ Tự* (The Famous Ancient Buddhist Temples in Vietnam).
5. *Hương Sen, Thơ và Nhạc* – (Lotus Fragrance, Poem and Music).
6. *Phật Giáo-Một Bậc Đạo Sư, Nhiều Truyền Thống* (Buddhism: One Teacher – Many Traditions), Đức Đạt Lai Lạt Ma 14th & Ni Sư Thubten Chodren.
7. *Cách Chuẩn Bị Chết và Giúp Người Sắp Chết-Quan Điểm Phật Giáo* (Preparing for Death and Helping the Dying – A Buddhist Perspective).

BUDDHIST MUSIC ALBUMS

from POEMS of THÍCH NỮ GIỚI HƯƠNG

1. *Đào Xuân Lộng Ý Kinh* (The Buddha's Teachings Reflected in Cherry Flowers).
2. *Niềm Tin Tam Bảo* (Trust in the Three Gems).
3. *Trăng Tròn Nghìn Năm Đón Chờ Ai* (Who Is the Full Moon Waiting for for Over a Thousand Years?).
4. *Ánh Trăng Phật Pháp (*Moonlight of Dharma-Buddha).
5. *Bình Minh Tỉnh Thức* (Awakened Mind at the Dawn) (*Piano Variations for Meditation*).
6. *Tiếng Hát Già Lam* (Song from Temple).
7. *Cảnh Đẹp Chùa Xưa* (The Magnificent, Ancient Buddhist Temple).
8. Karaoke *Hoa Ưu Đàm Đã Nở* (An Udumbara Flower Is Blooming).
9. *Hương Sen Ca* (Hương Sen's Songs).
10. *Về Chùa Vui Tu* (Happily Go to Temple for Spiritual Practices).
11. *Gọi Nắng Xuân Về* (Call the Spring Sunlight).
12. *Đệ Tử Phật* (The Buddha's Disciples).

Please consult the ***Bảo Anh Lạc Bookshelf*** *at this website:*

http://huongsentemple.com/index.php/en/about-us/b-o-anh-l-c-bookshelf

THE BLESSING CEREMONY FOR THE DECEASED

Author: Bao Anh Lac Bookshelf 69 - Huong Sen Buddhist Temple

HONG DUC PUBLISHING

Tel.: 024.39260024 - Fax : 024.39260031

Email: nhanxuatbanhongduc65@gmail.com

Responsible for publishing

Manager: **Bui Viet Bac**

Responsible for the content

Editor in Chief: **Ly Ba Toan**

Editor: **Phan Thi Ngoc Minh**

Presenter: **Vu Dinh Trong**

Editing the copy: **Vu Dinh Trong**

Printing quantity: 1,000 copies, Size: 14.5 x 20.5 cm

Printed at: Tram Anh Printing,

159/57 Bach Dang, Ward 2, Tan Binh District, HCM City.

Registration number:3214-2023/CXBIPH/39-92/HĐ

ISBN: 978-604-017-710-5

Publishing decision: 334/QD-NXBHD dated September 29, 2023

Finished printing and deposit in the third quarter of 2023

www.ingramcontent.com/pod-product-compliance
Lightning Source LLC
LaVergne TN
LVHW022319200926
848481LV00004B/1375